This Journal Belongs To

_____

Copyright © 2021 Purses & Proverbs

All rights reserved. No part of this book may be reproduced in any form or by any electronic or mechanical means, including information storage and retrieval systems, without permission in writing from the publisher, except by reviewers, who may quote brief passages in a review. Printed and bound in the United States of America

Website: https://www.pursesandproverbs.com/

How to Use This Journal

"It's never too late to become who you want to be. I hope you live a life that you're proud of, and if you find that you're not, I hope you have the strength to start over." — F. Scott Fitzgerald

Each and every day that you wake up, you are given another opportunity to make a decision to do and see things differently. Today, you've made the first decision in this journey by opening this journal.

Our hope is that as you remain consistent in writing these lists, you'll experience more joy, lessen any destructive habits, and gain more insight into who you are, where you are, and ultimately find yourself in the place you want to be.

What is the structure?
Each week you will be prompted with the same 5 topics in which you are asked to create a list as it pertains to the topic for that day. You will complete one (1) list each day (Monday-Friday), with 2 days for reflection (Saturday and Sunday). You will repeat this path every week.

Topics include:

- **Count Your Blessings**: This is your gratitude list; the things that you are thankful and grateful for.

- **No More Excuses**: What are the things you will start to do differently, instead of constantly making excuses for why you can't do them?

- **Be the Change**: What are the things that you will stop doing, that may be sabotaging your life in small or big ways?

- **You are Loved**: This list will give you permission to love your self. List all of the things that make you so special.

- **What do you see?**: This list will cause you to look at life through a different lens and cause you to really notice all of the good and beauty all around you.

- **Reflection**: There are two reflection lists; One to reflect on what you learned the past week, and the other to think about your expectations for the upcoming week.

- **Also included**: To-Do List, Journal pages, Savings Tracker, Habit Tracker, and Goal Tracker.

This page left blank intentionally

One Day Closer
7-Day Encouragement Audio

Scan the QR Code below to gain access to the audio companion to this planner.

The audio provides additional encouragement to take you through each of the 7 daily lists.

This page left blank intentionally

Key Definitions

"Understanding is the first step to acceptance, and only with acceptance can there be recovery." - J.K. Rowling

As you go through through this journey, there are several key words that you will see over and over again. Sometimes we use words, but are not really aware of the true definition of the words we use.

These key words are pulled from the introduction for each daily list. Refer to these definitions in order to gain clarity when writing your lists.

Thankful: feeling or expressing gratitude; appreciative.

Grateful: warmly or deeply appreciative of kindness or benefits received; thankful.

Excuses: to serve as an apology or justification for; justify.

Reflection: a fixing of the thoughts on something; careful consideration.

Intentional: done with intention or on purpose; intended;
an act or instance of determining mentally upon some action or result.

Blessings: a favor or gift bestowed by God, thereby bringing happiness.

Conscious: aware of what one is doing.

Change: to make the form, nature, content, future course, etc., of (something) different from what it is or from what it would be if left alone; to become different.

Habit: an acquired behavior pattern regularly followed until it has become almost involuntary.

This page left blank intentionally

Date:

Count Your Blessings

There is always, always, always, something to be thankful for.

We spend far too many days thinking about the things we *don't* have, when instead we should be thankful for the things we *do* have; the people, the experiences, the very breath we have that fuels our lives. Today, no matter what you're going through, count your blessings.

I Am So Thankful & Grateful For...

_____
_____
_____
_____
_____
_____
_____
_____
_____
_____
_____
_____
_____
_____
_____

Date:

No More Excuses
Today is the beginning of whatever you want

Date:

For whatever reason, we always seem to find an excuse for not doing the things that we know we should. Think about how far you could be 30 days, 6 months, or even 1 year from now, if you make today the day that you stop making excuses and just get started.

Today I Will Make a Conscious Choice To Start...

_____
_____
_____
_____
_____
_____
_____
_____
_____
_____
_____
_____
_____
_____

Date:

Date:

Be The Change

If you want things in your life to change, you have to change things in your life.

Just like we make excuses for why we don't do the things that we should, we also make excuses for why we continue to do the things that we shouldn't. Whether it's negative self-talk, or eating too much sugar, today is the day you can commit to do better; to be better.

Today I Will Make A Conscious Choice To Stop...

Date:

You Are Loved

Date:

Love yourself, because that's who you'll be spending the rest of your life with.

You are beautifully and wonderfully made; perfectly knitted in your mother's womb. You are beautiful, you are strong, you are a force to be reckoned with. YOU ARE ENOUGH!

Things I Love About Me...

_____
_____
_____
_____
_____
_____
_____
_____
_____
_____
_____
_____
_____
_____

Date:

Date:

What Do You See?

*People who see beauty all around them, live in a beautiful world.
People who see danger all around them, live in a dangerous world.
-Debasish Mridha*

If you spend your days immersed in the news of the day, you may have a jaded view of the world, but if you spend your days looking for the good things around you, you can experience a daily dose of joy. As you go about your day take the time to notice the good all around.

Good and Beautiful Things I Noticed Today...

_____
_____
_____
_____
_____
_____
_____
_____
_____
_____
_____
_____
_____
_____
_____

Date:

Date:

Reflection

Without reflection, we go blindly on our way, creating more unintended consequences, and failing to achieve anything useful ~Margaret J. Wheatley

Take some time to reflect on the last week. How did you feel as you completed each list? What went well? Where did you struggle?

As I reflect on this past week I discovered that...

_____
_____
_____
_____
_____
_____
_____
_____
_____
_____
_____
_____
_____
_____
_____
_____

Date:

Reflection

Date:

The best way to predict the future is to create it. ~Abraham Lincoln

Take some time to think about the coming week. In what ways will you commit to being intentional about your goals? What are you looking forward to this coming week?

Looking ahead at the coming week I will be intentional about...

Date:

Goal Trackr

A goal without a plan is just a dream.

GOALS	COMPLETE BY

Date:

Habit Tracker

Your habits will determine your future ~Jack Canfield

Implementing good habits starts with knowing the bad habits you want to change and replacing them with positive habits that will bring positive outcomes.

Positive Habits To Implement	M	T	W	T	F	S	S
_____	☐	☐	☐	☐	☐	☐	☐
_____	☐	☐	☐	☐	☐	☐	☐
_____	☐	☐	☐	☐	☐	☐	☐
_____	☐	☐	☐	☐	☐	☐	☐
_____	☐	☐	☐	☐	☐	☐	☐
_____	☐	☐	☐	☐	☐	☐	☐
_____	☐	☐	☐	☐	☐	☐	☐
_____	☐	☐	☐	☐	☐	☐	☐
_____	☐	☐	☐	☐	☐	☐	☐
_____	☐	☐	☐	☐	☐	☐	☐
_____	☐	☐	☐	☐	☐	☐	☐
_____	☐	☐	☐	☐	☐	☐	☐
_____	☐	☐	☐	☐	☐	☐	☐
_____	☐	☐	☐	☐	☐	☐	☐
_____	☐	☐	☐	☐	☐	☐	☐
_____	☐	☐	☐	☐	☐	☐	☐
_____	☐	☐	☐	☐	☐	☐	☐
_____	☐	☐	☐	☐	☐	☐	☐
_____	☐	☐	☐	☐	☐	☐	☐

Date:

Date:

Let's Do This!

To-Do List

o _____   o _____
o _____   o _____
o _____   o _____
o _____   o _____
o _____   o _____
o _____   o _____
o _____   o _____
o _____   o _____
o _____   o _____
o _____   o _____
o _____   o _____

Notes & Reminders

_____
_____
_____
_____
_____
_____
_____

Today is a good day to have a good day!

Date:

Date:

Count Your Blessings

There is always, always, always, something to be thankful for.

We spend far too many days thinking about the things we *don't* have, when instead we should be thankful for the things we *do* have; the people, the experiences, the very breath we have that fuels our lives. Today, no matter what you're going through, count your blessings.

I Am So Thankful & Grateful For...

Date:

No More Excuses

Date:

Today is the beginning of whatever you want

For whatever reason, we always seem to find an excuse for not doing the things that we know we should. Think about how far you could be 30 days, 6 months, or even 1 year from now, if you make today the day that you stop making excuses and just get started.

Today I Will Make a Conscious Choice To Start...

_____
_____
_____
_____
_____
_____
_____
_____
_____
_____
_____
_____
_____
_____
_____
_____

Date:

Date:

Be The Change

If you want things in your life to change, you have to change things in your life.

Just like we make excuses for why we don't do the things that we should, we also make excuses for why we continue to do the things that we shouldn't. Whether it's negative self-talk, or eating too much sugar, today is the day you can commit to do better; to be better.

Today I Will Make A Conscious Choice To Stop...

Date:

You Are Loved

Date:

Love yourself, because that's who you'll be spending the rest of your life with.

You are beautifully and wonderfully made; perfectly knitted in your mother's womb. You are beautiful, you are strong, you are a force to be reckoned with. YOU ARE ENOUGH!

Things I Love About Me...

Date:

Date:

What Do You See?

*People who see beauty all around them, live in a beautiful world.
People who see danger all around them, live in a dangerous world.
—Debasish Mridha*

If you spend your days immersed in the news of the day, you may have a jaded view of the world, but if you spend your days looking for the good things around you, you can experience a daily dose of joy. As you go about your day take the time to notice the good all around.

Good and Beautiful Things I Noticed Today...

_____
_____
_____
_____
_____
_____
_____
_____
_____
_____
_____
_____
_____
_____

Date:

Date:

Reflection

Without reflection, we go blindly on our way, creating more unintended consequences, and failing to achieve anything useful ~Margaret J. Wheatley

Take some time to reflect on the last week. How did you feel as you completed each list? What went well? Where did you struggle?

As I reflect on this past week I discovered that...

_____
_____
_____
_____
_____
_____
_____
_____
_____
_____
_____
_____
_____
_____
_____

Date:

Reflection

Date:

The best way to predict the future is to create it. ~Abraham Lincoln

Take some time to think about the coming week. In what ways will you commit to being intentional about your goals? What are you looking forward to this coming week?

Looking ahead at the coming week I will be intentional about...

_____
_____
_____
_____
_____
_____
_____
_____
_____
_____
_____
_____
_____
_____
_____

Date:

Goal Trackr

A goal without a plan is just a dream.

GOALS	COMPLETE BY

Date:

Habit Tracker

Your habits will determine your future ~Jack Canfield

Implementing good habits starts with knowing the bad habits you want to change and replacing them with positive habits that will bring positive outcomes.

Positive Habits To Implement

	M	T	W	T	F	S	S
_____	☐	☐	☐	☐	☐	☐	☐
_____	☐	☐	☐	☐	☐	☐	☐
_____	☐	☐	☐	☐	☐	☐	☐
_____	☐	☐	☐	☐	☐	☐	☐
_____	☐	☐	☐	☐	☐	☐	☐
_____	☐	☐	☐	☐	☐	☐	☐
_____	☐	☐	☐	☐	☐	☐	☐
_____	☐	☐	☐	☐	☐	☐	☐
_____	☐	☐	☐	☐	☐	☐	☐
_____	☐	☐	☐	☐	☐	☐	☐
_____	☐	☐	☐	☐	☐	☐	☐
_____	☐	☐	☐	☐	☐	☐	☐
_____	☐	☐	☐	☐	☐	☐	☐
_____	☐	☐	☐	☐	☐	☐	☐
_____	☐	☐	☐	☐	☐	☐	☐
_____	☐	☐	☐	☐	☐	☐	☐
_____	☐	☐	☐	☐	☐	☐	☐
_____	☐	☐	☐	☐	☐	☐	☐
_____	☐	☐	☐	☐	☐	☐	☐
_____	☐	☐	☐	☐	☐	☐	☐

Date:

Date:

Let's Do This!

To-Do List

o _____   o _____
o _____   o _____
o _____   o _____
o _____   o _____
o _____   o _____
o _____   o _____
o _____   o _____
o _____   o _____
o _____   o _____
o _____   o _____
o _____   o _____

Notes & Reminders

_____
_____
_____
_____
_____
_____
_____

Today is a good day to have a good day!

Date:

Date:

Count Your Blessings

There is always, always, always, something to be thankful for.

We spend far too many days thinking about the things we *don't* have, when instead we should be thankful for the things we *do* have; the people, the experiences, the very breath we have that fuels our lives. Today, no matter what you're going through, count your blessings.

I Am So Thankful & Grateful For...

_____
_____
_____
_____
_____
_____
_____
_____
_____
_____
_____
_____
_____
_____
_____
_____
_____

Date:

Date:

No More Excuses
Today is the beginning of whatever you want

For whatever reason, we always seem to find an excuse for not doing the things that we know we should. Think about how far you could be 30 days, 6 months, or even 1 year from now, if you make today the day that you stop making excuses and just get started.

Today I Will Make a Conscious Choice To Start...

Date:

Date:

Be The Change

If you want things in your life to change, you have to change things in your life.

Just like we make excuses for why we don't do the things that we should, we also make excuses for why we continue to do the things that we shouldn't. Whether it's negative self-talk, or eating too much sugar, today is the day you can commit to do better; to be better.

Today I Will Make A Conscious Choice To Stop...

_____
_____
_____
_____
_____
_____
_____
_____
_____
_____
_____
_____
_____
_____
_____

Date:

You Are Loved

Date:

Love yourself, because that's who you'll be spending the rest of your life with.

You are beautifully and wonderfully made; perfectly knitted in your mother's womb. You are beautiful, you are strong, you are a force to be reckoned with. YOU ARE ENOUGH!

Things I Love About Me...

_____

_____

_____

_____

_____

_____

_____

_____

_____

_____

_____

_____

_____

Date:

Date:

What Do You See?

People who see beauty all around them, live in a beautiful world.
People who see danger all around them, live in a dangerous world.
—Debasish Mridha

If you spend your days immersed in the news of the day, you may have a jaded view of the world, but if you spend your days looking for the good things around you, you can experience a daily dose of joy. As you go about your day take the time to notice the good all around.

Good and Beautiful Things I Noticed Today...

_____
_____
_____
_____
_____
_____
_____
_____
_____
_____
_____
_____
_____
_____
_____
_____
_____

Date:

Date:

Reflection

Without reflection, we go blindly on our way, creating more unintended consequences, and failing to achieve anything useful ~Margaret J. Wheatley

Take some time to reflect on the last week. How did you feel as you completed each list? What went well? Where did you struggle?

As I reflect on this past week I discovered that...

_____
_____
_____
_____
_____
_____
_____
_____
_____
_____
_____
_____
_____
_____

Date:

Reflection

Date:

The best way to predict the future is to create it. ~Abraham Lincoln

Take some time to think about the coming week. In what ways will you commit to being intentional about your goals? What are you looking forward to this coming week?

Looking ahead at the coming week I will be intentional about...

Date:

Goal Trackr

A goal without a plan is just a dream.

GOALS	COMPLETE BY

Date:

Habit Tracker

Your habits will determine your future ~Jack Canfield

Implementing good habits starts with knowing the bad habits you want to change and replacing them with positive habits that will bring positive outcomes.

Positive Habits To Implement

	M	T	W	T	F	S	S
_____	☐	☐	☐	☐	☐	☐	☐
_____	☐	☐	☐	☐	☐	☐	☐
_____	☐	☐	☐	☐	☐	☐	☐
_____	☐	☐	☐	☐	☐	☐	☐
_____	☐	☐	☐	☐	☐	☐	☐
_____	☐	☐	☐	☐	☐	☐	☐
_____	☐	☐	☐	☐	☐	☐	☐
_____	☐	☐	☐	☐	☐	☐	☐
_____	☐	☐	☐	☐	☐	☐	☐
_____	☐	☐	☐	☐	☐	☐	☐
_____	☐	☐	☐	☐	☐	☐	☐
_____	☐	☐	☐	☐	☐	☐	☐
_____	☐	☐	☐	☐	☐	☐	☐
_____	☐	☐	☐	☐	☐	☐	☐
_____	☐	☐	☐	☐	☐	☐	☐
_____	☐	☐	☐	☐	☐	☐	☐
_____	☐	☐	☐	☐	☐	☐	☐
_____	☐	☐	☐	☐	☐	☐	☐
_____	☐	☐	☐	☐	☐	☐	☐
_____	☐	☐	☐	☐	☐	☐	☐

Date:

Date:

Let's Do This!

To-Do List

o _____   o _____
o _____   o _____
o _____   o _____
o _____   o _____
o _____   o _____
o _____   o _____
o _____   o _____
o _____   o _____
o _____   o _____
o _____   o _____
o _____   o _____

Notes & Reminders

_____
_____
_____
_____
_____
_____
_____

Today is a good day to have a good day!

Date:

Date:

Count Your Blessings

There is always, always, always, something to be thankful for.

We spend far too many days thinking about the things we *don't* have, when instead we should be thankful for the things we *do* have; the people, the experiences, the very breath we have that fuels our lives. Today, no matter what you're going through, count your blessings.

I Am So Thankful & Grateful For...

_____
_____
_____
_____
_____
_____
_____
_____
_____
_____
_____
_____
_____
_____
_____
_____

Date:

Date:

No More Excuses
Today is the beginning of whatever you want

For whatever reason, we always seem to find an excuse for not doing the things that we know we should. Think about how far you could be 30 days, 6 months, or even 1 year from now, if you make today the day that you stop making excuses and just get started.

Today I Will Make a Conscious Choice To Start...

_____
_____
_____
_____
_____
_____
_____
_____
_____
_____
_____
_____
_____
_____
_____
_____
_____

Date:

Date:

Be The Change

If you want things in your life to change, you have to change things in your life.

Just like we make excuses for why we don't do the things that we should, we also make excuses for why we continue to do the things that we shouldn't. Whether it's negative self-talk, or eating too much sugar, today is the day you can commit to do better; to be better.

Today I Will Make A Conscious Choice To Stop...

_____
_____
_____
_____
_____
_____
_____
_____
_____
_____
_____
_____
_____
_____
_____
_____

Date:

You Are Loved

Date:

Love yourself, because that's who you'll be spending the rest of your life with.

You are beautifully and wonderfully made; perfectly knitted in your mother's womb. You are beautiful, you are strong, you are a force to be reckoned with. YOU ARE ENOUGH!

Things I Love About Me...

_____

_____

_____

_____

_____

_____

_____

_____

_____

_____

_____

_____

Date:

Date:

What Do You See?

People who see beauty all around them, live in a beautiful world.
People who see danger all around them, live in a dangerous world.
—Debasish Mridha

If you spend your days immersed in the news of the day, you may have a jaded view of the world, but if you spend your days looking for the good things around you, can experience a daily dose of joy. As you go about your day take the time to notice the good all around.

Good and Beautiful Things I Noticed Today...

_____
_____
_____
_____
_____
_____
_____
_____
_____
_____
_____
_____
_____
_____
_____
_____

Date:

Date:

Reflection

Without reflection, we go blindly on our way, creating more unintended consequences, and failing to achieve anything useful ~Margaret J. Wheatley

Take some time to reflect on the last week. How did you feel as you completed each list? What went well? Where did you struggle?

As I reflect on this past week I discovered that...

Date:

Reflection

Date:

The best way to predict the future is to create it. ~Abraham Lincoln

Take some time to think about the coming week. In what ways will you commit to being intentional about your goals? What are you looking forward to this coming week?

Looking ahead at the coming week I will be intentional about...

Date:

Goal Trackr

A goal without a plan is just a dream.

GOALS	COMPLETE BY

Date:

Habit Tracker

Your habits will determine your future ~Jack Canfield

Implementing good habits starts with knowing the bad habits you want to change and replacing them with positive habits that will bring positive outcomes.

Positive Habits To Implement

	M	T	W	T	F	S	S
_____	☐	☐	☐	☐	☐	☐	☐
_____	☐	☐	☐	☐	☐	☐	☐
_____	☐	☐	☐	☐	☐	☐	☐
_____	☐	☐	☐	☐	☐	☐	☐
_____	☐	☐	☐	☐	☐	☐	☐
_____	☐	☐	☐	☐	☐	☐	☐
_____	☐	☐	☐	☐	☐	☐	☐
_____	☐	☐	☐	☐	☐	☐	☐
_____	☐	☐	☐	☐	☐	☐	☐
_____	☐	☐	☐	☐	☐	☐	☐
_____	☐	☐	☐	☐	☐	☐	☐
_____	☐	☐	☐	☐	☐	☐	☐
_____	☐	☐	☐	☐	☐	☐	☐
_____	☐	☐	☐	☐	☐	☐	☐
_____	☐	☐	☐	☐	☐	☐	☐
_____	☐	☐	☐	☐	☐	☐	☐
_____	☐	☐	☐	☐	☐	☐	☐
_____	☐	☐	☐	☐	☐	☐	☐
_____	☐	☐	☐	☐	☐	☐	☐
_____	☐	☐	☐	☐	☐	☐	☐

Date:

Date:

Let's Do This!

To-Do List

o _____   o _____
o _____   o _____
o _____   o _____
o _____   o _____
o _____   o _____
o _____   o _____
o _____   o _____
o _____   o _____
o _____   o _____
o _____   o _____
o _____   o _____

Notes & Reminders

_____
_____
_____
_____
_____
_____
_____

Today is a good day to have a good day!

Date:

Date:

Count Your Blessings

There is always, always, always, something to be thankful for.

We spend far too many days thinking about the things we *don't* have, when instead we should be thankful for the things we *do* have; the people, the experiences, the very breath we have that fuels our lives. Today, no matter what you're going through, count your blessings.

I Am So Thankful & Grateful For...

_____
_____
_____
_____
_____
_____
_____
_____
_____
_____
_____
_____
_____
_____
_____
_____
_____
_____

Date:

No More Excuses

Today is the beginning of whatever you want

Date:

For whatever reason, we always seem to find an excuse for not doing the things that we know we should. Think about how far you could be 30 days, 6 months, or even 1 year from now, if you make today the day that you stop making excuses and just get started.

Today I Will Make a Conscious Choice To Start...

_____
_____
_____
_____
_____
_____
_____
_____
_____
_____
_____
_____
_____
_____

Date:

Be The Change

Date:

If you want things in your life to change, you have to change things in your life.

Just like we make excuses for why we don't do the things that we should, we also make excuses for why we continue to do the things that we shouldn't. Whether it's negative self-talk, or eating too much sugar, today is the day you can commit to do better; to be better.

Today I Will Make A Conscious Choice To Stop...

_____
_____
_____
_____
_____
_____
_____
_____
_____
_____
_____
_____
_____
_____

Date:

You Are Loved

Love yourself, because that's who you'll be spending the rest of your life with.

Date:

You are beautifully and wonderfully made; perfectly knitted in your mother's womb. You are beautiful, you are strong, you are a force to be reckoned with. YOU ARE ENOUGH!

Things I Love About Me...

_____

_____

_____

_____

_____

_____

_____

_____

_____

_____

_____

_____

Date:

Date:

What Do You See?

People who see beauty all around them, live in a beautiful world.
People who see danger all around them, live in a dangerous world.
—Debasish Mridha

If you spend your days immersed in the news of the day, you may have a jaded view of the world, but if you spend your days looking for the good things around you, can experience a daily dose of joy. As you go about your day take the time to notice the good all around.

Good and Beautiful Things I Noticed Today...

_____
_____
_____
_____
_____
_____
_____
_____
_____
_____
_____
_____
_____
_____
_____

Date:

Date:

Reflection

Without reflection, we go blindly on our way, creating more unintended consequences, and failing to achieve anything useful ~Margaret J. Wheatley

Take some time to reflect on the last week. How did you feel as you completed each list? What went well? Where did you struggle?

As I reflect on this past week I discovered that...

Date:

Reflection

Date:

The best way to predict the future is to create it. ~Abraham Lincoln

Take some time to think about the coming week. In what ways will you commit to being intentional about your goals? What are you looking forward to this coming week?

Looking ahead at the coming week I will be intentional about...

_____
_____
_____
_____
_____
_____
_____
_____
_____
_____
_____
_____
_____
_____
_____
_____
_____

Date:

Goal Tracker

A goal without a plan is just a dream.

GOALS	COMPLETE BY

Date:

Habit Tracker

Your habits will determine your future ~Jack Canfield

Implementing good habits starts with knowing the bad habits you want to change and replacing them with positive habits that will bring positive outcomes.

Positive Habits To Implement	M	T	W	T	F	S	S
_____	☐	☐	☐	☐	☐	☐	☐
_____	☐	☐	☐	☐	☐	☐	☐
_____	☐	☐	☐	☐	☐	☐	☐
_____	☐	☐	☐	☐	☐	☐	☐
_____	☐	☐	☐	☐	☐	☐	☐
_____	☐	☐	☐	☐	☐	☐	☐
_____	☐	☐	☐	☐	☐	☐	☐
_____	☐	☐	☐	☐	☐	☐	☐
_____	☐	☐	☐	☐	☐	☐	☐
_____	☐	☐	☐	☐	☐	☐	☐
_____	☐	☐	☐	☐	☐	☐	☐
_____	☐	☐	☐	☐	☐	☐	☐
_____	☐	☐	☐	☐	☐	☐	☐
_____	☐	☐	☐	☐	☐	☐	☐
_____	☐	☐	☐	☐	☐	☐	☐
_____	☐	☐	☐	☐	☐	☐	☐
_____	☐	☐	☐	☐	☐	☐	☐
_____	☐	☐	☐	☐	☐	☐	☐
_____	☐	☐	☐	☐	☐	☐	☐

Date:

Date:

Let's Do This!

To-Do List

o _____   o _____
o _____   o _____
o _____   o _____
o _____   o _____
o _____   o _____
o _____   o _____
o _____   o _____
o _____   o _____
o _____   o _____
o _____   o _____
o _____   o _____

Notes & Reminders

_____
_____
_____
_____
_____
_____
_____

Today is a good day to have a good day!

Date:

Date:

Count Your Blessings

There is always, always, always, something to be thankful for.

We spend far too many days thinking about the things we *don't* have, when instead we should be thankful for the things we *do* have; the people, the experiences, the very breath we have that fuels our lives. Today, no matter what you're going through, count your blessings.

I Am So Thankful & Grateful For...

Date:

No More Excuses

Today is the beginning of whatever you want

Date:

For whatever reason, we always seem to find an excuse for not doing the things that we know we should. Think about how far you could be 30 days, 6 months, or even 1 year from now, if you make today the day that you stop making excuses and just get started.

Today I Will Make a Conscious Choice To Start...

_____
_____
_____
_____
_____
_____
_____
_____
_____
_____
_____
_____
_____
_____
_____
_____
_____
_____
_____
_____

Date:

Date:

Be The Change

If you want things in your life to change, you have to change things in your life.

Just like we make excuses for why we don't do the things that we should, we also make excuses for why we continue to do the things that we shouldn't. Whether it's negative self-talk, or eating too much sugar, today is the day you can commit to do better; to be better.

Today I Will Make A Conscious Choice To Stop...

_____
_____
_____
_____
_____
_____
_____
_____
_____
_____
_____
_____
_____
_____
_____

Date:

You Are Loved

Date:

Love yourself, because that's who you'll be spending the rest of your life with.

You are beautifully and wonderfully made; perfectly knitted in your mother's womb. You are beautiful, you are strong, you are a force to be reckoned with. YOU ARE ENOUGH!

Things I Love About Me...

_____
_____
_____
_____
_____
_____
_____
_____
_____
_____
_____
_____
_____
_____
_____
_____

Date:

Date:

What Do You See?

People who see beauty all around them, live in a beautiful world.
People who see danger all around them, live in a dangerous world.
—Debasish Mridha

If you spend your days immersed in the news of the day, you may have a jaded view of the world, but if you spend your days looking for the good things around you, you can experience a daily dose of joy. As you go about your day take the time to notice the good all around.

Good and Beautiful Things I Noticed Today...

_____
_____
_____
_____
_____
_____
_____
_____
_____
_____
_____
_____
_____
_____

Date:

Date:

Reflection

Without reflection, we go blindly on our way, creating more unintended consequences, and failing to achieve anything useful ~Margaret J. Wheatley

Take some time to reflect on the last week. How did you feel as you completed each list? What went well? Where did you struggle?

As I reflect on this past week I discovered that...

_____
_____
_____
_____
_____
_____
_____
_____
_____
_____
_____
_____
_____
_____
_____

Date:

Reflection

Date:

The best way to predict the future is to create it. ~Abraham Lincoln

Take some time to think about the coming week. In what ways will you commit to being intentional about your goals? What are you looking forward to this coming week?

Looking ahead at the coming week I will be intentional about...

Date:

Goal Trackr

A goal without a plan is just a dream.

GOALS	COMPLETE BY

Date:

Habit Tracker

Your habits will determine your future ~Jack Canfield

Implementing good habits starts with knowing the bad habits you want to change and replacing them with positive habits that will bring positive outcomes.

Positive Habits To Implement

	M	T	W	T	F	S	S
_____	☐	☐	☐	☐	☐	☐	☐
_____	☐	☐	☐	☐	☐	☐	☐
_____	☐	☐	☐	☐	☐	☐	☐
_____	☐	☐	☐	☐	☐	☐	☐
_____	☐	☐	☐	☐	☐	☐	☐
_____	☐	☐	☐	☐	☐	☐	☐
_____	☐	☐	☐	☐	☐	☐	☐
_____	☐	☐	☐	☐	☐	☐	☐
_____	☐	☐	☐	☐	☐	☐	☐
_____	☐	☐	☐	☐	☐	☐	☐
_____	☐	☐	☐	☐	☐	☐	☐
_____	☐	☐	☐	☐	☐	☐	☐
_____	☐	☐	☐	☐	☐	☐	☐
_____	☐	☐	☐	☐	☐	☐	☐
_____	☐	☐	☐	☐	☐	☐	☐
_____	☐	☐	☐	☐	☐	☐	☐
_____	☐	☐	☐	☐	☐	☐	☐
_____	☐	☐	☐	☐	☐	☐	☐
_____	☐	☐	☐	☐	☐	☐	☐

Date:

Date:

Let's Do This!

To-Do List

o _____   o _____
o _____   o _____
o _____   o _____
o _____   o _____
o _____   o _____
o _____   o _____
o _____   o _____
o _____   o _____
o _____   o _____
o _____   o _____
o _____   o _____

Notes & Reminders

_____
_____
_____
_____
_____
_____
_____

Today is a good day to have a good day!

Date:

Date:

Count Your Blessings

There is always, always, always, something to be thankful for.

We spend far too many days thinking about the things we *don't* have, when instead we should be thankful for the things we *do* have; the people, the experiences, the very breath we have that fuels our lives. Today, no matter what you're going through, count your blessings.

I Am So Thankful & Grateful For...

_____
_____
_____
_____
_____
_____
_____
_____
_____
_____
_____
_____
_____
_____
_____
_____
_____

Date:

No More Excuses

Today is the beginning of whatever you want

Date:

For whatever reason, we always seem to find an excuse for not doing the things that we know we should. Think about how far you could be 30 days, 6 months, or even 1 year from now, if you make today the day that you stop making excuses and just get started.

Today I Will Make a Conscious Choice To Start...

_____

_____

_____

_____

_____

_____

_____

_____

_____

_____

_____

_____

Date:

Date:

Be The Change

If you want things in your life to change, you have to change things in your life.

Just like we make excuses for why we don't do the things that we should, we also make excuses for why we continue to do the things that we shouldn't. Whether it's negative self-talk, or eating too much sugar, today is the day you can commit to do better; to be better.

Today I Will Make A Conscious Choice To Stop...

_____
_____
_____
_____
_____
_____
_____
_____
_____
_____
_____
_____
_____
_____
_____
_____

Date:

You Are Loved

Date:

Love yourself, because that's who you'll be spending the rest of your life with.

You are beautifully and wonderfully made; perfectly knitted in your mother's womb. You are beautiful, you are strong, you are a force to be reckoned with. YOU ARE ENOUGH!

Things I Love About Me...

Date:

Date:

What Do You See?

People who see beauty all around them, live in a beautiful world.
People who see danger all around them, live in a dangerous world.
—Debasish Mridha

If you spend your days immersed in the news of the day, you may have a jaded view of the world, but if you spend your days looking for the good things around you, you can experience a daily dose of joy. As you go about your day take the time to notice the good all around.

Good and Beautiful Things I Noticed Today...

_____
_____
_____
_____
_____
_____
_____
_____
_____
_____
_____
_____
_____
_____
_____

Date:

Reflection

Date:

Without reflection, we go blindly on our way, creating more unintended consequences, and failing to achieve anything useful ~Margaret J. Wheatley

Take some time to reflect on the last week. How did you feel as you completed each list? What went well? Where did you struggle?

As I reflect on this past week I discovered that...

Date:

Reflection

Date:

The best way to predict the future is to create it. ~Abraham Lincoln

Take some time to think about the coming week. In what ways will you commit to being intentional about your goals? What are you looking forward to this coming week?

Looking ahead at the coming week I will be intentional about...

Date:

Goal Tracker

A goal without a plan is just a dream.

GOALS	COMPLETE BY

Date:

Habit Tracker

Your habits will determine your future ~Jack Canfield

Implementing good habits starts with knowing the bad habits you want to change and replacing them with positive habits that will bring positive outcomes.

Positive Habits To Implement

	M	T	W	T	F	S	S
___	☐	☐	☐	☐	☐	☐	☐
___	☐	☐	☐	☐	☐	☐	☐
___	☐	☐	☐	☐	☐	☐	☐
___	☐	☐	☐	☐	☐	☐	☐
___	☐	☐	☐	☐	☐	☐	☐
___	☐	☐	☐	☐	☐	☐	☐
___	☐	☐	☐	☐	☐	☐	☐
___	☐	☐	☐	☐	☐	☐	☐
___	☐	☐	☐	☐	☐	☐	☐
___	☐	☐	☐	☐	☐	☐	☐
___	☐	☐	☐	☐	☐	☐	☐
___	☐	☐	☐	☐	☐	☐	☐
___	☐	☐	☐	☐	☐	☐	☐
___	☐	☐	☐	☐	☐	☐	☐
___	☐	☐	☐	☐	☐	☐	☐
___	☐	☐	☐	☐	☐	☐	☐
___	☐	☐	☐	☐	☐	☐	☐
___	☐	☐	☐	☐	☐	☐	☐
___	☐	☐	☐	☐	☐	☐	☐

Date:

Date:

Let's Do This!

To-Do List

- o _____
- o _____
- o _____
- o _____
- o _____
- o _____
- o _____
- o _____
- o _____
- o _____
- o _____

- o _____
- o _____
- o _____
- o _____
- o _____
- o _____
- o _____
- o _____
- o _____
- o _____
- o _____

Notes & Reminders

_____
_____
_____
_____
_____
_____
_____
_____

Today is a good day to have a good day!

Date:

Date:

Count Your Blessings

There is always, always, always, something to be thankful for.

We spend far too many days thinking about the things we *don't* have, when instead we should be thankful for the things we *do* have; the people, the experiences, the very breath we have that fuels our lives. Today, no matter what you're going through, count your blessings.

I Am So Thankful & Grateful For...

_____

_____

_____

_____

_____

_____

_____

_____

_____

_____

_____

_____

_____

_____

Date:

No More Excuses

Today is the beginning of whatever you want

Date:

For whatever reason, we always seem to find an excuse for not doing the things that we know we should. Think about how far you could be 30 days, 6 months, or even 1 year from now, if you make today the day that you stop making excuses and just get started.

Today I Will Make a Conscious Choice To Start...

_____
_____
_____
_____
_____
_____
_____
_____
_____
_____
_____
_____
_____
_____
_____

Date:

Date:

Be The Change

If you want things in your life to change, you have to change things in your life.

Just like we make excuses for why we don't do the things that we should, we also make excuses for why we continue to do the things that we shouldn't. Whether it's negative self-talk, or eating too much sugar, today is the day you can commit to do better; to be better.

Today I Will Make A Conscious Choice To Stop...

_____
_____
_____
_____
_____
_____
_____
_____
_____
_____
_____
_____
_____
_____
_____
_____

Date:

Date:

You Are Loved

Love yourself, because that's who you'll be spending the rest of your life with.

You are beautifully and wonderfully made; perfectly knitted in your mother's womb. You are beautiful, you are strong, you are a force to be reckoned with. YOU ARE ENOUGH!

Things I Love About Me...

_____
_____
_____
_____
_____
_____
_____
_____
_____
_____
_____
_____

Date:

Date:

What Do You See?

*People who see beauty all around them, live in a beautiful world.
People who see danger all around them, live in a dangerous world.
—Debasish Mridha*

If you spend your days immersed in the news of the day, you may have a jaded view of the world, but if you spend your days looking for the good things around you, you can experience a daily dose of joy. As you go about your day take the time to notice the good all around.

Good and Beautiful Things I Noticed Today...

_____
_____
_____
_____
_____
_____
_____
_____
_____
_____
_____
_____

Date:

Date:

Reflection

Without reflection, we go blindly on our way, creating more unintended consequences, and failing to achieve anything useful ~Margaret J. Wheatley

Take some time to reflect on the last week. How did you feel as you completed each list? What went well? Where did you struggle?

As I reflect on this past week I discovered that...

_____
_____
_____
_____
_____
_____
_____
_____
_____
_____
_____
_____
_____
_____

Date:

Reflection

The best way to predict the future is to create it. ~Abraham Lincoln

Date:

Take some time to think about the coming week. In what ways will you commit to being intentional about your goals? What are you looking forward to this coming week?

Looking ahead at the coming week I will be intentional about...

Date:

Goal Tracker

A goal without a plan is just a dream.

GOALS	COMPLETE BY

Date:

Habit Tracker

Your habits will determine your future ~Jack Canfield

Implementing good habits starts with knowing the bad habits you want to change and replacing them with positive habits that will bring positive outcomes.

Positive Habits To Implement

	M	T	W	T	F	S	S
_____	☐	☐	☐	☐	☐	☐	☐
_____	☐	☐	☐	☐	☐	☐	☐
_____	☐	☐	☐	☐	☐	☐	☐
_____	☐	☐	☐	☐	☐	☐	☐
_____	☐	☐	☐	☐	☐	☐	☐
_____	☐	☐	☐	☐	☐	☐	☐
_____	☐	☐	☐	☐	☐	☐	☐
_____	☐	☐	☐	☐	☐	☐	☐
_____	☐	☐	☐	☐	☐	☐	☐
_____	☐	☐	☐	☐	☐	☐	☐
_____	☐	☐	☐	☐	☐	☐	☐
_____	☐	☐	☐	☐	☐	☐	☐
_____	☐	☐	☐	☐	☐	☐	☐
_____	☐	☐	☐	☐	☐	☐	☐
_____	☐	☐	☐	☐	☐	☐	☐
_____	☐	☐	☐	☐	☐	☐	☐
_____	☐	☐	☐	☐	☐	☐	☐
_____	☐	☐	☐	☐	☐	☐	☐
_____	☐	☐	☐	☐	☐	☐	☐

Date:

Date:

Let's Do This!

To-Do List

o _____   o _____
o _____   o _____
o _____   o _____
o _____   o _____
o _____   o _____
o _____   o _____
o _____   o _____
o _____   o _____
o _____   o _____
o _____   o _____
o _____   o _____

Notes & Reminders

_____
_____
_____
_____
_____
_____
_____
_____

Today is a good day to have a good day!

Date:

Date:

Count Your Blessings

There is always, always, always, something to be thankful for.

We spend far too many days thinking about the things we *don't* have, when instead we should be thankful for the things we *do* have; the people, the experiences, the very breath we have that fuels our lives. Today, no matter what you're going through, count your blessings.

I Am So Thankful & Grateful For...

_____
_____
_____
_____
_____
_____
_____
_____
_____
_____
_____
_____
_____
_____
_____

Date:

No More Excuses
Today is the beginning of whatever you want

Date:

For whatever reason, we always seem to find an excuse for not doing the things that we know we should. Think about how far you could be 30 days, 6 months, or even 1 year from now, if you make today the day that you stop making excuses and just get started.

Today I Will Make a Conscious Choice To Start...

_____

_____

_____

_____

_____

_____

_____

_____

_____

_____

_____

_____

_____

Date:

Be The Change

Date:

If you want things in your life to change, you have to change things in your life.

Just like we make excuses for why we don't do the things that we should, we also make excuses for why we continue to do the things that we shouldn't. Whether it's negative self-talk, or eating too much sugar, today is the day you can commit to do better; to be better.

Today I Will Make A Conscious Choice To Stop...

_____

_____

_____

_____

_____

_____

_____

_____

_____

_____

_____

_____

_____

Date:

You Are Loved

Date:

Love yourself, because that's who you'll be spending the rest of your life with.

You are beautifully and wonderfully made; perfectly knitted in your mother's womb. You are beautiful, you are strong, you are a force to be reckoned with. YOU ARE ENOUGH!

Things I Love About Me...

_____
_____
_____
_____
_____
_____
_____
_____
_____
_____
_____
_____
_____

Date:

Date:

What Do You See?

People who see beauty all around them, live in a beautiful world.
People who see danger all around them, live in a dangerous world.
—Debasish Mridha

If you spend your days immersed in the news of the day, you may have a jaded view of the world, but if you spend your days looking for the good things around you, can experience a daily dose of joy. As you go about your day take the time to notice the good all around.

Good and Beautiful Things I Noticed Today...

_____
_____
_____
_____
_____
_____
_____
_____
_____
_____
_____
_____
_____

Date:

Date:

Reflection

Without reflection, we go blindly on our way, creating more unintended consequences, and failing to achieve anything useful ~Margaret J. Wheatley

Take some time to reflect on the last week. How did you feel as you completed each list? What went well? Where did you struggle?

As I reflect on this past week I discovered that...

Date:

Reflection

Date:

The best way to predict the future is to create it. ~Abraham Lincoln

Take some time to think about the coming week. In what ways will you commit to being intentional about your goals? What are you looking forward to this coming week?

Looking ahead at the coming week I will be intentional about...

_____
_____
_____
_____
_____
_____
_____
_____
_____
_____
_____
_____
_____
_____
_____
_____

Date:

Goal Trackr

A goal without a plan is just a dream.

GOALS	COMPLETE BY

Date:

Habit Tracker

Your habits will determine your future ~Jack Canfield

Implementing good habits starts with knowing the bad habits you want to change and replacing them with positive habits that will bring positive outcomes.

Positive Habits To Implement

	M	T	W	T	F	S	S
_____	☐	☐	☐	☐	☐	☐	☐
_____	☐	☐	☐	☐	☐	☐	☐
_____	☐	☐	☐	☐	☐	☐	☐
_____	☐	☐	☐	☐	☐	☐	☐
_____	☐	☐	☐	☐	☐	☐	☐
_____	☐	☐	☐	☐	☐	☐	☐
_____	☐	☐	☐	☐	☐	☐	☐
_____	☐	☐	☐	☐	☐	☐	☐
_____	☐	☐	☐	☐	☐	☐	☐
_____	☐	☐	☐	☐	☐	☐	☐
_____	☐	☐	☐	☐	☐	☐	☐
_____	☐	☐	☐	☐	☐	☐	☐
_____	☐	☐	☐	☐	☐	☐	☐
_____	☐	☐	☐	☐	☐	☐	☐
_____	☐	☐	☐	☐	☐	☐	☐
_____	☐	☐	☐	☐	☐	☐	☐
_____	☐	☐	☐	☐	☐	☐	☐
_____	☐	☐	☐	☐	☐	☐	☐
_____	☐	☐	☐	☐	☐	☐	☐

Date:

Date:

Let's Do This!

To-Do List

o _____   o _____
o _____   o _____
o _____   o _____
o _____   o _____
o _____   o _____
o _____   o _____
o _____   o _____
o _____   o _____
o _____   o _____
o _____   o _____
o _____   o _____

Notes & Reminders

_____
_____
_____
_____
_____
_____
_____

Today is a good day to have a good day!

Date:

Date:

Count Your Blessings

There is always, always, always, something to be thankful for.

We spend far too many days thinking about the things we *don't* have, when instead we should be thankful for the things we *do* have; the people, the experiences, the very breath we have that fuels our lives. Today, no matter what you're going through, count your blessings.

I Am So Thankful & Grateful For...

Date:

No More Excuses
Today is the beginning of whatever you want

Date:

For whatever reason, we always seem to find an excuse for not doing the things that we know we should. Think about how far you could be 30 days, 6 months, or even 1 year from now, if you make today the day that you stop making excuses and just get started.

Today I Will Make a Conscious Choice To Start...

_____

_____

_____

_____

_____

_____

_____

_____

_____

_____

_____

_____

_____

_____

Date:

Date:

Be The Change

If you want things in your life to change, you have to change things in your life.

Just like we make excuses for why we don't do the things that we should, we also make excuses for why we continue to do the things that we shouldn't. Whether it's negative self-talk, or eating too much sugar, today is the day you can commit to do better; to be better.

Today I Will Make A Conscious Choice To Stop...

_____
_____
_____
_____
_____
_____
_____
_____
_____
_____
_____
_____
_____
_____
_____
_____

Date:

You Are Loved

Date:

Love yourself, because that's who you'll be spending the rest of your life with.

You are beautifully and wonderfully made; perfectly knitted in your mother's womb. You are beautiful, you are strong, you are a force to be reckoned with. YOU ARE ENOUGH!

Things I Love About Me...

_____
_____
_____
_____
_____
_____
_____
_____
_____
_____
_____
_____
_____

Date:

Date:

What Do You See?

*People who see beauty all around them, live in a beautiful world.
People who see danger all around them, live in a dangerous world.
—Debasish Mridha*

If you spend your days immersed in the news of the day, you may have a jaded view of the world, but if you spend your days looking for the good things around you, can experience a daily dose of joy. As you go about your day take the time to notice the good all around.

Good and Beautiful Things I Noticed Today...

_____
_____
_____
_____
_____
_____
_____
_____
_____
_____
_____
_____
_____
_____

Date:

Date:

Reflection

Without reflection, we go blindly on our way, creating more unintended consequences, and failing to achieve anything useful ~Margaret J. Wheatley

Take some time to reflect on the last week. How did you feel as you completed each list? What went well? Where did you struggle?

As I reflect on this past week I discovered that...

_____
_____
_____
_____
_____
_____
_____
_____
_____
_____
_____
_____
_____
_____
_____

Date:

Reflection

Date:

The best way to predict the future is to create it. ~Abraham Lincoln

Take some time to think about the coming week. In what ways will you commit to being intentional about your goals? What are you looking forward to this coming week?

Looking ahead at the coming week I will be intentional about...

_____
_____
_____
_____
_____
_____
_____
_____
_____
_____
_____
_____
_____
_____
_____

Date:

Goal Tracker

A goal without a plan is just a dream.

GOALS	COMPLETE BY

Date:

Habit Tracker

Your habits will determine your future ~Jack Canfield

Implementing good habits starts with knowing the bad habits you want to change and replacing them with positive habits that will bring positive outcomes.

Positive Habits To Implement

	M	T	W	T	F	S	S
_____	☐	☐	☐	☐	☐	☐	☐
_____	☐	☐	☐	☐	☐	☐	☐
_____	☐	☐	☐	☐	☐	☐	☐
_____	☐	☐	☐	☐	☐	☐	☐
_____	☐	☐	☐	☐	☐	☐	☐
_____	☐	☐	☐	☐	☐	☐	☐
_____	☐	☐	☐	☐	☐	☐	☐
_____	☐	☐	☐	☐	☐	☐	☐
_____	☐	☐	☐	☐	☐	☐	☐
_____	☐	☐	☐	☐	☐	☐	☐
_____	☐	☐	☐	☐	☐	☐	☐
_____	☐	☐	☐	☐	☐	☐	☐
_____	☐	☐	☐	☐	☐	☐	☐
_____	☐	☐	☐	☐	☐	☐	☐
_____	☐	☐	☐	☐	☐	☐	☐
_____	☐	☐	☐	☐	☐	☐	☐
_____	☐	☐	☐	☐	☐	☐	☐
_____	☐	☐	☐	☐	☐	☐	☐
_____	☐	☐	☐	☐	☐	☐	☐
_____	☐	☐	☐	☐	☐	☐	☐

Date:

Date:

Let's Do This!

To-Do List

o _____   o _____
o _____   o _____
o _____   o _____
o _____   o _____
o _____   o _____
o _____   o _____
o _____   o _____
o _____   o _____
o _____   o _____
o _____   o _____
o _____   o _____

Notes & Reminders

_____
_____
_____
_____
_____
_____
_____
_____

Today is a good day to have a good day!

Date:

Date:

Count Your Blessings

There is always, always, always, something to be thankful for.

We spend far too many days thinking about the things we *don't* have, when instead we should be thankful for the things we *do* have; the people, the experiences, the very breath we have that fuels our lives. Today, no matter what you're going through, count your blessings.

I Am So Thankful & Grateful For...

_____
_____
_____
_____
_____
_____
_____
_____
_____
_____
_____
_____
_____
_____
_____
_____
_____

Date:

No More Excuses
Today is the beginning of whatever you want

Date:

For whatever reason, we always seem to find an excuse for not doing the things that we know we should. Think about how far you could be 30 days, 6 months, or even 1 year from now, if you make today the day that you stop making excuses and just get started.

Today I Will Make a Conscious Choice To Start...

_____

_____

_____

_____

_____

_____

_____

_____

_____

_____

_____

_____

_____

Date:

Date:

Be The Change

If you want things in your life to change, you have to change things in your life.

Just like we make excuses for why we don't do the things that we should, we also make excuses for why we continue to do the things that we shouldn't. Whether it's negative self-talk, or eating too much sugar, today is the day you can commit to do better; to be better.

Today I Will Make A Conscious Choice To Stop...

_____
_____
_____
_____
_____
_____
_____
_____
_____
_____
_____
_____
_____
_____
_____
_____
_____
_____
_____

Date:

You Are Loved

Date:

Love yourself, because that's who you'll be spending the rest of your life with.

You are beautifully and wonderfully made; perfectly knitted in your mother's womb. You are beautiful, you are strong, you are a force to be reckoned with. YOU ARE ENOUGH!

Things I Love About Me...

_____
_____
_____
_____
_____
_____
_____
_____
_____
_____
_____
_____
_____
_____

Date:

Date:

What Do You See?

People who see beauty all around them, live in a beautiful world.
People who see danger all around them, live in a dangerous world.
—Debasish Mridha

If you spend your days immersed in the news of the day, you may have a jaded view of the world, but if you spend your days looking for the good things around you, you can experience a daily dose of joy. As you go about your day take the time to notice the good all around.

Good and Beautiful Things I Noticed Today...

_____
_____
_____
_____
_____
_____
_____
_____
_____
_____
_____
_____
_____
_____
_____

Date:

Date:

Reflection

Without reflection, we go blindly on our way, creating more unintended consequences, and failing to achieve anything useful ~Margaret J. Wheatley

Take some time to reflect on the last week. How did you feel as you completed each list? What went well? Where did you struggle?

As I reflect on this past week I discovered that...

_____
_____
_____
_____
_____
_____
_____
_____
_____
_____
_____
_____
_____
_____
_____

Date:

Reflection

Date:

The best way to predict the future is to create it. ~Abraham Lincoln

Take some time to think about the coming week. In what ways will you commit to being intentional about your goals? What are you looking forward to this coming week?

Looking ahead at the coming week I will be intentional about...

Date:

Goal Tracker

A goal without a plan is just a dream.

GOALS	COMPLETE BY

Date:

Habit Tracker

Your habits will determine your future ~Jack Canfield

Implementing good habits starts with knowing the bad habits you want to change and replacing them with positive habits that will bring positive outcomes.

Positive Habits To Implement	M	T	W	T	F	S	S
_____	☐	☐	☐	☐	☐	☐	☐
_____	☐	☐	☐	☐	☐	☐	☐
_____	☐	☐	☐	☐	☐	☐	☐
_____	☐	☐	☐	☐	☐	☐	☐
_____	☐	☐	☐	☐	☐	☐	☐
_____	☐	☐	☐	☐	☐	☐	☐
_____	☐	☐	☐	☐	☐	☐	☐
_____	☐	☐	☐	☐	☐	☐	☐
_____	☐	☐	☐	☐	☐	☐	☐
_____	☐	☐	☐	☐	☐	☐	☐
_____	☐	☐	☐	☐	☐	☐	☐
_____	☐	☐	☐	☐	☐	☐	☐
_____	☐	☐	☐	☐	☐	☐	☐
_____	☐	☐	☐	☐	☐	☐	☐
_____	☐	☐	☐	☐	☐	☐	☐
_____	☐	☐	☐	☐	☐	☐	☐
_____	☐	☐	☐	☐	☐	☐	☐
_____	☐	☐	☐	☐	☐	☐	☐
_____	☐	☐	☐	☐	☐	☐	☐
_____	☐	☐	☐	☐	☐	☐	☐

Date:

Date:

Let's Do This!

To-Do List

o _____   o _____
o _____   o _____
o _____   o _____
o _____   o _____
o _____   o _____
o _____   o _____
o _____   o _____
o _____   o _____
o _____   o _____
o _____   o _____
o _____   o _____

Notes & Reminders

_____
_____
_____
_____
_____
_____
_____
_____

Today is a good day to have a good day!

Date:

Date:

Count Your Blessings

There is always, always, always, something to be thankful for.

We spend far too many days thinking about the things we *don't* have, when instead we should be thankful for the things we *do* have; the people, the experiences, the very breath we have that fuels our lives. Today, no matter what you're going through, count your blessings.

I Am So Thankful & Grateful For...

_____
_____
_____
_____
_____
_____
_____
_____
_____
_____
_____
_____
_____
_____
_____
_____

Date:

No More Excuses

Today is the beginning of whatever you want

Date:

For whatever reason, we always seem to find an excuse for not doing the things that we know we should. Think about how far you could be 30 days, 6 months, or even 1 year from now, if you make today the day that you stop making excuses and just get started.

Today I Will Make a Conscious Choice To Start...

_____

_____

_____

_____

_____

_____

_____

_____

_____

_____

_____

_____

_____

Date:

Date:

Be The Change

If you want things in your life to change, you have to change things in your life.

Just like we make excuses for why we don't do the things that we should, we also make excuses for why we continue to do the things that we shouldn't. Whether it's negative self-talk, or eating too much sugar, today is the day you can commit to do better; to be better.

Today I Will Make A Conscious Choice To Stop...

Date:

You Are Loved

Date:

Love yourself, because that's who you'll be spending the rest of your life with.

You are beautifully and wonderfully made; perfectly knitted in your mother's womb. You are beautiful, you are strong, you are a force to be reckoned with. YOU ARE ENOUGH!

Things I Love About Me...

_____
_____
_____
_____
_____
_____
_____
_____
_____
_____
_____
_____
_____
_____

Date:

Date:

What Do You See?

*People who see beauty all around them, live in a beautiful world.
People who see danger all around them, live in a dangerous world.*
—Debasish Mridha

If you spend your days immersed in the news of the day, you may have a jaded view of the world, but if you spend your days looking for the good things around you, you can experience a daily dose of joy. As you go about your day take the time to notice the good all around.

Good and Beautiful Things I Noticed Today...

_____
_____
_____
_____
_____
_____
_____
_____
_____
_____
_____
_____
_____
_____

Date:

Date:

Reflection

Without reflection, we go blindly on our way, creating more unintended consequences, and failing to achieve anything useful ~Margaret J. Wheatley

Take some time to reflect on the last week. How did you feel as you completed each list? What went well? Where did you struggle?

As I reflect on this past week I discovered that...

_____
_____
_____
_____
_____
_____
_____
_____
_____
_____
_____
_____
_____
_____
_____

Date:

Reflection

Date:

The best way to predict the future is to create it. ~Abraham Lincoln

Take some time to think about the coming week. In what ways will you commit to being intentional about your goals? What are you looking forward to this coming week?

Looking ahead at the coming week I will be intentional about...

_____
_____
_____
_____
_____
_____
_____
_____
_____
_____
_____
_____
_____
_____

Date:

Goal Tracker

A goal without a plan is just a dream.

GOALS	COMPLETE BY

Date:

Habit Tracker

Your habits will determine your future ~Jack Canfield

Implementing good habits starts with knowing the bad habits you want to change and replacing them with positive habits that will bring positive outcomes.

Positive Habits To Implement

	M	T	W	T	F	S	S
	☐	☐	☐	☐	☐	☐	☐
	☐	☐	☐	☐	☐	☐	☐
	☐	☐	☐	☐	☐	☐	☐
	☐	☐	☐	☐	☐	☐	☐
	☐	☐	☐	☐	☐	☐	☐
	☐	☐	☐	☐	☐	☐	☐
	☐	☐	☐	☐	☐	☐	☐
	☐	☐	☐	☐	☐	☐	☐
	☐	☐	☐	☐	☐	☐	☐
	☐	☐	☐	☐	☐	☐	☐
	☐	☐	☐	☐	☐	☐	☐
	☐	☐	☐	☐	☐	☐	☐
	☐	☐	☐	☐	☐	☐	☐
	☐	☐	☐	☐	☐	☐	☐
	☐	☐	☐	☐	☐	☐	☐
	☐	☐	☐	☐	☐	☐	☐
	☐	☐	☐	☐	☐	☐	☐
	☐	☐	☐	☐	☐	☐	☐
	☐	☐	☐	☐	☐	☐	☐

Date:

Date:

Let's Do This!

To-Do List

o _____ o _____
o _____ o _____
o _____ o _____
o _____ o _____
o _____ o _____
o _____ o _____
o _____ o _____
o _____ o _____
o _____ o _____
o _____ o _____
o _____ o _____

Notes & Reminders

_____
_____
_____
_____
_____
_____
_____
_____

Today is a good day to have a good day!

Date:

Date:

Count Your Blessings

There is always, always, always, something to be thankful for.

We spend far too many days thinking about the things we *don't* have, when instead we should be thankful for the things we *do* have; the people, the experiences, the very breath we have that fuels our lives. Today, no matter what you're going through, count your blessings.

I Am So Thankful & Grateful For...

_____

_____

_____

_____

_____

_____

_____

_____

_____

_____

_____

_____

_____

Date:

No More Excuses

Today is the beginning of whatever you want

Date:

For whatever reason, we always seem to find an excuse for not doing the things that we know we should. Think about how far you could be 30 days, 6 months, or even 1 year from now, if you make today the day that you stop making excuses and just get started.

Today I Will Make a Conscious Choice To Start...

_____
_____
_____
_____
_____
_____
_____
_____
_____
_____
_____
_____

Date:

Date:

Be The Change

If you want things in your life to change, you have to change things in your life.

Just like we make excuses for why we don't do the things that we should, we also make excuses for why we continue to do the things that we shouldn't. Whether it's negative self-talk, or eating too much sugar, today is the day you can commit to do better; to be better.

Today I Will Make A Conscious Choice To Stop...

_____
_____
_____
_____
_____
_____
_____
_____
_____
_____
_____
_____
_____
_____

Date:

You Are Loved

Love yourself, because that's who you'll be spending the rest of your life with.

You are beautifully and wonderfully made; perfectly knitted in your mother's womb. You are beautiful, you are strong, you are a force to be reckoned with. YOU ARE ENOUGH!

Things I Love About Me...

Date:

Date:

What Do You See?

Date:

*People who see beauty all around them, live in a beautiful world.
People who see danger all around them, live in a dangerous world.
-Debasish Mridha*

If you spend your days immersed in the news of the day, you may have a jaded view of the world, but if you spend your days looking for the good things around you, you can experience a daily dose of joy. As you go about your day take the time to notice the good all around.

Good and Beautiful Things I Noticed Today...

_____
_____
_____
_____
_____
_____
_____
_____
_____
_____
_____
_____
_____
_____
_____
_____
_____

Date:

Date:

Reflection

Without reflection, we go blindly on our way, creating more unintended consequences, and failing to achieve anything useful ~Margaret J. Wheatley

Take some time to reflect on the last week. How did you feel as you completed each list? What went well? Where did you struggle?

As I reflect on this past week I discovered that...

_____
_____
_____
_____
_____
_____
_____
_____
_____
_____
_____
_____
_____
_____
_____

Date:

Date:

Reflection

The best way to predict the future is to create it. ~Abraham Lincoln

Take some time to think about the coming week. In what ways will you commit to being intentional about your goals? What are you looking forward to this coming week?

Looking ahead at the coming week I will be intentional about...

_____
_____
_____
_____
_____
_____
_____
_____
_____
_____
_____
_____
_____
_____

Date:

Goal Trackr

A goal without a plan is just a dream.

GOALS	COMPLETE BY

Date:

Habit Tracker

Your habits will determine your future ~Jack Canfield

Implementing good habits starts with knowing the bad habits you want to change and replacing them with positive habits that will bring positive outcomes.

Positive Habits To Implement	M	T	W	T	F	S	S
_____	☐	☐	☐	☐	☐	☐	☐
_____	☐	☐	☐	☐	☐	☐	☐
_____	☐	☐	☐	☐	☐	☐	☐
_____	☐	☐	☐	☐	☐	☐	☐
_____	☐	☐	☐	☐	☐	☐	☐
_____	☐	☐	☐	☐	☐	☐	☐
_____	☐	☐	☐	☐	☐	☐	☐
_____	☐	☐	☐	☐	☐	☐	☐
_____	☐	☐	☐	☐	☐	☐	☐
_____	☐	☐	☐	☐	☐	☐	☐
_____	☐	☐	☐	☐	☐	☐	☐
_____	☐	☐	☐	☐	☐	☐	☐
_____	☐	☐	☐	☐	☐	☐	☐
_____	☐	☐	☐	☐	☐	☐	☐
_____	☐	☐	☐	☐	☐	☐	☐
_____	☐	☐	☐	☐	☐	☐	☐
_____	☐	☐	☐	☐	☐	☐	☐
_____	☐	☐	☐	☐	☐	☐	☐
_____	☐	☐	☐	☐	☐	☐	☐
_____	☐	☐	☐	☐	☐	☐	☐

Date:

Date:

Let's Do This!

To-Do List

- o _____
- o _____
- o _____
- o _____
- o _____
- o _____
- o _____
- o _____
- o _____
- o _____
- o _____

- o _____
- o _____
- o _____
- o _____
- o _____
- o _____
- o _____
- o _____
- o _____
- o _____
- o _____

Notes & Reminders

_____
_____
_____
_____
_____
_____
_____
_____

Today is a good day to have a good day!

Date:

Savings Tracker

SAVING FOR	START	END	GOAL $

DATE	DEPOSIT $	MEMO	BALANCE $

Date:

Savings Tracker

SAVING FOR		START	END	GOAL $

DATE	DEPOSIT $	MEMO	BALANCE $

Date:

Savings Tracker

SAVING FOR		START	END	GOAL $

DATE	DEPOSIT $	MEMO	BALANCE $

Date:

Savings Tracker

SAVING FOR		START	END	GOAL $

DATE	DEPOSIT $	MEMO	BALANCE $

Date:

Savings Tracker

SAVING FOR		START	END	GOAL $

DATE	DEPOSIT $	MEMO	BALANCE $

Date:

Date:

Date:

Date:

Date:

Date:

Date:

Date:

Date:

Date:

Date:

Date:

www.ingramcontent.com/pod-product-compliance
Lightning Source LLC
Chambersburg PA
CBHW080726230426
43665CB00020B/2639